POWERPOINT DOESN'T SUCK, YOU DO

The counter-intuitive approach
to compelling presentations.

Dear Kathy,
Thanks for being
part of my network.
I hope you enjoy!
Dave ☺

David McGimpsey

CONTENTS

A poor craftsman blames his tools.

INTRODUCTION

My first ever presentation was a train wreck.

Let me tell you what happened.

Years ago, I worked for an extremely dysfunctional organization. The atmosphere in my department was toxic. People were burned-out and unhappy with the working conditions of the office, interpersonal politics were insane, and projects were stalled. Nothing was getting done fast. It was a "professional" war zone. As hard as they might have tried, the management couldn't get things moving in the right direction.

I was relatively new and had no ax to grind with any members of the department. Although it wasn't comfortable, I could go about my day without getting involved in any politics or getting into screaming matches. Being quite new, and not being a member of any particular group, I could observe what was going on objectively. I could see what was happening around me and I could clearly identify the root cause of some of the problems. I took notes and kept my head down.

Things were so bad that, over a few weeks, my notes had substantial information that could be put to good use. As I reviewed them, I could see recurring themes and problems, which could be resolved with a few tweaks here and there. The closer I looked at my notes, the clearer the solution became. I sat down, and I drafted out a plan. A plan to improve the work environment. A plan which would neutralize the bad apples, make the office a better place to work, increase efficiency, and make our department more profitable. If I could fix these problems, even a little, it would surely be good for my career, so I worked hard on my plan.

It took about two weeks of observation and late nights, but I had my plan! I was exhausted, but it was ready. Just a tweak here and a tiny adjustment there, and the cogs would be spinning smoothly in the department again. The plan was good to go, but I had a problem. If I wanted to get my plan implemented, I would need to present the details to the management to get their buy-in. Without them on my side, my plan was going nowhere.

So, I recommitted myself to the long hours, and I hit PowerPoint hard. I doubled down on the long nights, putting together my charts and bullet points, aligning my images and text. I practiced my lines in front of the mirror, while walking the dog, and on the train. After another week of late nights, skipped meals, and pots of coffee, I had a gleaming slide deck, a practiced speech, and a whole lot of butterflies in my stomach. I was nervous but ready. I had a solid plan, and that's all that mattered.

The day came. The management team filed into meeting room 6 and waited. I was about to take the stage, but the nerves got the better of me. Something was holding me back. I looked out into the audience and saw managers whispering to each and shifting uncomfortably on the hard chairs. I only had one chance to get this right. I closed my eyes, took a deep breath, and walked out onto the small platform. I stood in front of them shaking. Slides behind me, laser pointer in one hand, cue cards in other. I froze! What was I meant to say? I'd practiced and practiced and practiced, but no words would come. My legs started to shake, and I could feel the blood rush to my face.

More uncomfortable shifting from the managers. I stared at them. They stared back at me. Waiting for this to be over. One manager kindly asked me if I needed some water, another very deliberately checked his watch as if to say, "You're wasting my time, buddy." My mind was racing. Madly trying to reach back and remember some of my practice. Oh, why couldn't I remember? It seemed the more I tried to remember, the further away the memories became.

I glanced down at the cards in my hand. Seeing the keywords made things even more confusing, more blockades of my memories. One gentleman stood up as if to leave. I had to do something! This idea was going to save my department! Then I remembered... My slides! This was my only chance. I flicked on the slides, turned around, and began reading the bullet points from slide 1 to the managers.

By the second slide, the tension in the room had started to lift, and I was getting into the swing of things. Some memories were coming back, which made speaking about my bullet points a little easier. The process of reading a bullet point and elaborating went on for some time.

It was around slide number 6 that I realized that the room was dead silent. I took my eyes off my slides and checked the audience behind me. No one was paying attention! They were checking their messages, writing, one manager was even reading a magazine. I spun back around and read through the remainder of the slides and bullet points as quickly as I could.

Five minutes later I handed over the stage to the audience for questions. Nothing. Silence. No questions. "Come on!" I thought. "Ask me some questions. This is an amazing plan.

A fantastic idea that will make this a better workplace for everyone, increase efficiency, and make us more money."

Blank stares mixed with silence. My eyes pleaded with the audience for what felt like minutes.

Finally, at the back of the room, someone raised their hand. My heart lifted, and I extended my hand in his direction. "Yes sir, you have a question?"

"Can we go now please?"

And there you have it. My first presentation. A nightmare.

Since then I do things differently. I have discovered what works, and what definitely does not work, when delivering a presentation.

In the following pages, I will share my secrets with you.

Are you ready? Okay! Onward and upward!

David McGimpsey
Osaka, Japan

. . . . . ● . . . .

I have good news and bad news. Both involve your slide deck.

Let's start with the bad.

Those PowerPoint slides? The ones that you're working so hard on? Yeah, they're not going to help your presentation.

Worse still, that PowerPoint template. The one that you paid good money for. It won't make a speck of difference to the reception, or retention, of your message.

Want proof?

Imagine a slide deck from a Steve Jobs presentation delivered by Barry from accounting.

The bad news is, we see PowerPoint as both the problem and solution. And it is neither. PowerPoint (or Keynote or Prezi) is just a tool. A tool which can be used well or used badly. Sadly, in most cases, it is used badly to support a bad presentation delivery. And this brings me to the good news.

You can deliver an awesome presentation! It's simpler than you imagine and, even if all your presentations to date have been shockers, you can do it. It's most likely easier than how you're going about your presentations now. And you can do it with or without the support of PowerPoint.

You see, a good presentation has nothing to do with PowerPoint and everything to do with you. Get the "you" right, and the slides become almost irrelevant. Get the "you" right, and you can deliver a confident, engaging presentation.

This book is all about how you can get the "you" right. The simple ways to improve your delivery to engage your audience, get them to buy-in to your ideas, and get them to take action.

Important note: Before we go any further it is important that I point out that I have no issues with PowerPoint. Any reference to PowerPoint you find throughout this text could be easily replaced with Keynote or Prezi. I reference PowerPoint in this text because it is the product which has become synonymous with the slide deck.

PART ONE

THE SLAP

J erry wiped the sweat from his top lip.

He was only half-listening to his colleagues.

As Greg and Max chatted about office politics, Jerry focused on very different matters.

Today had been a rip-roaring success. Jerry, Greg, and Max had finally closed the high dollar deal they'd been working on for the last six months. The ink on the client contract was still drying while the trio began their celebrations.

Greg nudged Jerry, "Want another beer?"

Jerry nodded absentmindedly. Greg headed to the bar for refills. Max hit the bathroom.

Alone, Jerry was able to focus. He took the crumpled cue cards from his jacket pocket and shuffled through them.

Each cue card contained three items. Among the items on the cards were opening lines and talking points. Jerry had prepared the dog-eared mess a couple of weeks earlier. The only exercise they'd seen so far was a laundry spin cycle.

Jerry was a success in business but unsuccessful in love. He could close deals, implement projects, manage people, keep work conflict under control. He could even convince hordes of staff to accept an unpopular change initiative. But he couldn't get himself a girlfriend.

Even the thought of approaching a woman made Jerry tongue-tied. Unable to think of what to say. His approachees would watch Jerry with sympathy as he mumbled sounds and foamed at the mouth. Sympathy quickly changed to irritation as his prospects worked out that he wasn't actually a simpleton but that this was a pickup attempt. Tonight was going to be different, he thought. Tonight, he would be confident. He just needed to find a nice girl to approach.

The bar was filling up now. Greg was still waiting to be served. Max was still in line for the bathroom.

Jerry scanned the dark room, occasionally fanning rogue tobacco smoke away from his face. And he finally saw her. Sitting at a small table in the corner. All by herself. In the darkness. Sipping a cocktail and checking her phone. She was very cute and appeared to be alone.

Jerry was suddenly filled with panic. This was her! This was his chance! His moment!

He had to act now! He had been here before, and lost out due to inaction. Time spent getting siked up in similar situations before had resulted in missed opportunities; Jerry usurped by more eager approachers.

He stood and reached for his cue cards. Ripping them from his jacket pocket, he knocked his glass over. The glass hit the ground with a thud but mercifully didn't break. Presumably, the sticky carpet provided a soft landing. A spatter of beer dripped from Jerry's crotch.

He looked up, red-faced. Had anyone noticed? It appeared not. The ambient noise of the bar had swallowed this accident. Jerry grabbed some napkins and gingerly patted his crotch dry.

She was talking on her phone now. Perhaps organizing to meet someone later. He needed to act fast. Get over this fear and just act! Jerry consulted his cue cards one last time. He repeated the lines to himself, closed his eyes, and stepped forward. There was no going back.

Greg returned with beer to find their seats abandoned and Jerry's glass and chair overturned.

Jerry moved slowly and purposefully towards the alcove. His legs felt like dead weights, but he pushed forward. He was almost there now, committed. It was now more embarrassing to turn back than to continue. He pinched his cue cards tightly, pressed against his arm, and protruding from the left cuff of his shirt.

He was within reach of her table now. She sensed his presence and looked up, then quickly looked back down at her phone.

Jerry's mouth was dry. He was sure no words would come out.

He was there. He stood motionless for a second. After what seemed like minutes she looked up. *Come on cue cards*, he thought.

"What's up?" she asked.

Jerry's mind was racing. He needed to say something! She was already starting to recoil at this long silence.

He stuttered like the ignition of old car. And then the words finally came. *Yay, cue cards!*

"I would like to date you." She recoiled further. Jerry noticed and sped things along.

"There are 3 things I want to talk to you about. First, I'd like to discuss our hobbies and interests. Second, we should talk about dating history, and... erm..." Jerry let the cue cards slip a little from his sleeve and glanced quickly, "oh... finally, we should discuss where to go on our first date."

Jerry paused and waited for a response. Nothing. She just sat, mouth open, phone still in her hand.

He continued, "So, if you don't have any questions at this stage, why don't we talk about your hobbies?"

As Jerry reached for the chair next to her, she stood up quickly and shoved him away from the chair. "What are you doing, creep?"

Jerry was caught off balance. In an effort to protect his precious cue cards from being discovered, he wobbled and slipped forward. Now he was falling towards his "target". She let out a scream and slapped Jerry across the face.

Jerry continued his forward trajectory and landed on the floor.

Greg and Max arrived just in time to see the object of Jerry's affections storming away.

· · · · ● ● · · · ·

So, here's what just happened. Jerry got very unlucky. He tried to do what he thought was right and failed miserably. His deep-seated fear of rejection caused him to plan in such way that failure was inevitable.

He wanted desperately to get a date, and he set about preparing to get one.

His preparation was all wrong. He prepared to reach his goal as quickly as possible, i.e., *How can I get a date in as few steps as possible?* The pattern he followed was probably something like this:

1. I want to get a date as quickly and painlessly as possible

2. I fear the possibility of rejection and negative judgment

3. I will probably forget what to say or run out of things to say, so...

4. I will write talking points on cue cards in order to have an easy reference when I am out and about

5. I will practice reading the talking points, confident that if I forget something, I can check the cue cards anytime

First, Jerry is never going to get a date. Second, he is making this way too difficult for himself. He is setting up an interaction where he needs to do all the work, which the other party won't be interested in anyway.

Jerry is so focused on his goal that he is not considering anything about the relationship. In Jerry's mind, the relationship is secondary to fulfilling his goal: *Get the date and worry about the relationship part later.* The trouble for Jerry is that no one is going to listen to him, let alone agree to go out on a date with him.

Let's consider what would have happened if Jerry had taken a different approach. No cue cards. No rehearsing of talking points. Instead, Jerry starts with a simple "Hello". He asks some questions, actually listens to the answers, and starts to build a rapport between himself and the lady. In turn, she might ask Jerry some questions. Very soon they have introduced themselves and the rapport continues to build.

Jerry still might not get a date, but he has a much better chance.

So, what's the point of all this, and how does it relate to presentations? All in all, Jerry just did what we all do in our presentations every day!

If we change the scenery a little bit and replay the events around Jerry's proposition, what we can see is the same pattern we use every day at work or at school.

1. I want to get through my presentation as quickly and painlessly as possible

2. I fear the possibility of rejection and negative judgment

3. I will probably forget what to say or run out of things to say, so...

4. I will start with PowerPoint (or Keynote or Prezi) and type out my headings and bullet points in order to have an easy reference when I am delivering my presentation

5. I will practice reading the bullet points, confident that if I forget something I can refer to the slides anytime

This is how most of us prepare presentations. And we all know what it's like to be in the audience with a presenter who has prepared this way. This is the very reason we pay so little attention to presentations. This is why we walk out of presentations with very little new knowledge. This is why we dread going to the next presentation.

But if we started our preparation with PowerPoint, isn't that the problem?

You can certainly blame PowerPoint, or whatever slide software you used, for a bad presentation. Blaming the software escapes the real issue. The real issue is you. The real issue is your inability to connect with your audience and build a rapport with them; to frame your topic in a way where the audience understands why it is important and pays attention because they want to, not because they have to.

To succeed in work, business, and life, communication is key. Develop your communication skills in a way that captures your listeners' attention, engages them, and leads them to action. If you can do that, bullet points are irrelevant. This book is a self-contained guide about how to stop blaming PowerPoint and how to develop your presentation skills to push you ahead in your business, your career, and your life.

the roof! Think about this: If you go to a doctor and ask for a diagnosis about a problem you've been having and the doctor turns around and punches your symptoms into Google, you're going to have some doubts when you get the eventual diagnosis. If, however, he speaks confidently while he gathers information, looks you in the eye, and doesn't spin around to consult WedMD, you're much more likely to believe him and trust his diagnosis.

It enhances the purpose of your slides. The original purpose of slides, way back in the days of overhead projectors, was to support the speech of the presenter, not to overtake it. Unfortunately, "presentation" has become synonymous with "slides". Using the goal-driven approach to presentations, you return slides to their original purpose. This enhances their effectiveness as a signpost of what the presenter is saying.

It permits the audience to pay attention. While the presenter talks and the slides display a list of bullet points, what is the audience to do? They try to listen while also trying to read the bullets. The audience's focus is divided, and the result is that little is retained from the presentation. With the goal-driven approach, the need for the slides to cue what the presenter is saying is removed. The audience can focus on listening, questioning, and understanding. The likely result is that the audience retains more.

DRAWBACKS OF THE GOAL-DRIVEN APPROACH

It requires contemplation. For the goal-driven approach to be effective, you can't jump in and start building slides; you can't start writing a script cold. The goal-driven approach requires that you start by getting an understanding of your audience and their preferences. It requires that you think about the main themes of your talk. And it requires that you gain a deep understanding of your subject matter (if you don't have one already). While the goal-driven approach takes the same amount of work, or can even save time, overall, the fact that the initial stages are not spent producing content can be scary for presenters.

It goes against what we do by default. From the first presentation you have observed in business or at school, it is clear how the presentation was put together: slides first. It is natural, therefore, that when you need to deliver your first presentation, you start from the slides. In a time when everyone is walking around with at least one smart device or computer on them, it's natural for us to seek out software to begin the process of solving a problem. Additionally, when you're preparing for a presentation, the organizer will often request that you show them your slides in advance to know what you are going to say. As we will see later in this book, it's just another reason we naturally start work with PowerPoint, and this is something you should push back on.

It may not be right for your business. In certain businesses, it may not be appropriate to spend time trying to engage your audience. At first, this may sound strange. Why would an audience not want to be engaged with a topic? Why would an audience not want the presenter to try and capture their attention so they can easily understand the presentation contents? The answer comes down to "ceremony." There are some businesses where presentations are treated simply as ceremony or stage-gating. This is the idea that you can't progress with your project until you've done a presentation or reported out. You simply have to prove you've done "the work" by standing in front of a group of stakeholders and reading some bullet points to them. This point shouldn't dissuade you from doing a goal-driven presentation. Just remember that if you work in a business like this, you may face some resistance to your goal-driven presentation. But who knows, you might change the culture of the business for the better.

WHICH APPROACH IS BEST?

There is no right or wrong approach. Whether you choose a slide-driven approach or goal-driven approach, or some hybrid, depends entirely on your situation at the time.

WHEN TO SELECT THE SLIDE-DRIVEN APPROACH

Are you time poor and need to get a presentation for delivery on a tight deadline? Will you have no time to practice? Are you not confident in your knowledge about your subject matter and don't have time to become familiar with it? If you answered "yes" to any of these questions, a slide-driven approach to your presentation could be most suitable.

WHEN TO SELECT THE GOAL-DRIVEN APPROACH

Are you delivering a sales presentation? Are you delivering a presentation where you need to be persuasive and achieve some kind of buy-in? Are you delivering a presentation to a skeptical audience? Are you delivering a presentation that matters in some way to your career? Are you delivering a presentation where you have to introduce a change? If you answered "yes" to any of these questions, then you are probably going to have the most success with the goal-driven approach.

WHEN TO SELECT NEITHER OPTION

Before settling on either of the approaches, you should first ask yourself if you need to use either of them. Do you know your subject matter well enough that you've got no preparation to do at all? Is this more of a discussion than a formal presentation? Would a whiteboard and marker be sufficient? Are slides just going to get in the way of a fluid discussion? Remember that many productive business discussions have been destroyed with the introduction of formality and slides. Framing what could be a presentation as a discussion could make it much easier to introduce an idea and have it accepted. It's much easier to keep a group of people engaged when there's the potential for the back and forth of ideas. For the presenter/facilitator, the task is less daunting then a proper presentation because a discussion doesn't come with the same baggage. You may get more engagement from the meeting where you give a short subject matter summary (presentation) coupled with whiteboard or flipchart (slides), followed by a discussion or brainstorming session (Q&A).

THE PROBLEM AND SOLUTION TO PRESENTATIONS

There's a fundamental issue with presentations. The people doing them don't want to do them. The people listening to them don't want to listen to them. Unless there is a shift in our thinking, presentations will continue to be the black sheep of business.

Presentations are not going anywhere, so there needs to be a better way of dealing with them than we currently do. The answer lies in looking at how we communicate with each other socially. Social communication is far more effective than business communication. We are more easily able to engage the people we are talking with. We are more easily able to be persuasive. The question then becomes, what are we doing socially that's more effective than what we are doing in business?

We could do a lot of experiments to work out why social communication tends to be more effective than business communication, however the easiest way is to take a regular social interaction and imagine how it would be handled in business. To do this, all we need to do is add pressure. Pressure is the key difference and key problem.

Let's take a step back to Jerry's comical efforts to find a date in the bar. Jerry made a mess of his interaction because there was a business element involved. Some pressure. Jerry needed to "close the deal" and get the date. There was a risk of rejection.

Let's remove the pressure. Imagine Jerry has a steady girlfriend. He's in the same bar after work with the same work mates. Max goes for beer, Greg heads to the bathroom. Jerry looks up and notices the same beautiful lady sitting in the corner. He's not looking for date, so there is no pressure. He decides to go over and say hello. Jerry will go over without a second thought, without feeling the need to check his cue cards. Why? Because the pressure's not there. He's not looking for a date, he just wants someone to chat with. If she rejects his introduction, so what? Jerry can go and talk to someone else. The pressure is absent.

Let's look at a different example. You are at a social dinner chatting with some friends. The conversation suddenly reminds you of a funny incident that happened last week. You tell the story to your friends. As you relay the story, you speak smoothly, confidently. You don't worry about forgetting parts of the story and you don't beat yourself up if you do. You don't worry about mistakes or people judging you, you just tell the story. While you talk, your friends remain engaged.

Why does this conversation go so smoothly? Several reasons. You're among friends, there's no pressure, and you're talking about a subject that you know well and you don't require a prompting device to help you. Removing pressure lends itself to a confident, smooth, engaging delivery of a message.

Imagine the same conversation being delivered with bullet point slides. Would the story be as fluid? Would the listeners be able to pay full attention to what you are saying? Even though you know the subject matter well, would you be able to keep your eyes from straying towards the slides?

Our best chance at removing pressure and delivering a smooth, confident, engaging presentation is to use the goal-driven approach. When we take this approach to presentations, we shift our focus from slides and on to the content.

In the coming chapters we'll look at the steps you need to follow to successfully use the goal-driven approach.

3

POURING THE CEMENT

P reparation is perhaps the most important part of anything you do. The solid foundation you lay during the preparation phase supports the book you will write, the project you will manage, or the presentation you will deliver.

When you fail to plan, you plan to fail.

When you take a vacation, you don't jump in the car, drive to the airport, and then think, "Which country should I go to for vacation?" That would be a nightmare. Imagine the many problems you'd encounter. Vacationing in the wrong season, missing prime holiday events in your chosen vacation spot, stores and hotspots closed because of the time of year, hotels booked out or closed for the off-season. Instead, by planning in advance, creating an itinerary, and pre-booking what you need, vacations go relatively smoothly.

If we can do this with vacations, why can't we do this planning with our presentations? There are probably many reasons, but one that springs to mind is that a presentation is too easy to do wrong. For instance, a vacation abroad is extremely expensive. If we do no preparation and the vacation ends up being a disaster, we lose a lot of money. There's a cost barrier that forces us to think. Starting a business is even more expensive, and there's a huge risk that even a business that has had initial success will still fail. To reduce the chance of failure, we do our research and prepare cautiously. When it comes to presentations, in all but limited situations, the "cost barrier" is not there. If we do a bad presentation and bore our audience, no one dies and no one's out of pocket an extreme amount of money. It could be argued that bad presentations waste businesses lots of money every year, but individual presenters aren't thinking about that. They're concerned solely with getting off the stage as quickly as possible.

So, if there are no immediate consequences for doing a crappy presentation and it means the time spent on preparation can be avoided, why should a presenter prepare? Well, there are no immediate, visible consequences for doing a bad presentation, but that doesn't mean that there are no long-term ones. Do you really want to be known as the worst presenter in your firm? Do you really want attendees joining your delivery purely out of duty? Remember also that being able to speak about your ideas and responsibilities in a confident, clear, and persuasive manner is often a pre-requisite for promotion. Strong communication skills will serve you well as you begin the move into different positions within your company or when you choose to move on to bigger and better things.

If I take the slide-driven approach and begin by preparing my PowerPoint slides, isn't that classed as preparation? Yes, it is, but think about it like this. Imagine building a house. You build the frame of the roof, put all the roof tiles on and then lay the foundations. It's backwards, and you're going to have to do a lot of extra work to get the roof on once the foundations and frame are fixed. Start with your slides in your presentation, and it's like building the roof of a house first.

The order you prepare your presentation may not follow this exact path, but I recommend this flow as a starting point:

1. Decide what the take-away is for the audience;

2. If there is part of your presentation you are not sure about, start learning, start getting familiar with it;

3. Make a basic outline of your presentation (not a script);

4. Frame your outline and take-away for the audience;

5. Commence practice. Practice talking about each of the points in your presentation until you have a cohesive speech that you can deliver without prompts like notes and cue cards;

6. Video-tape yourself and watch it back with a critical eye. Address only the two biggest problem areas you found, no more;

7. Time permitting, repeat step 6;

8. Build your slides. At this point, use your latest video recording and only create slides which emphasize key points in your speech; and

9. Practice your speech again with slides. At this stage, your focus should be on not looking at the slides as you talk (this should be easy because you've already got your speech under control).

PART TWO

4

CHOOSE YOUR DESTINATION

Richard Smith had worked at Capital Finance for ten years. In those ten years, he had always been an adviser. His popularity with his clients had increased year on year. Richard's name came up somewhere in every year-end awards ceremony as the employee who got the most new business, or the team member with the best client feedback, or some such achievement. Richard's skills and rapport with customers were highly valued in his firm, and he demanded a high salary in return.

Today marked one of the rare occasions where Richard found himself out of his depth. He was scheduled to deliver a presentation. To a large audience. To all junior advisers at Capital Finance. The hope was that Richard could impart some nuggets of wisdom to the junior members of the team to begin developing some mini-Richards. While retirement was many years off, the partners at the firm recognized that building their business on Richard's talents alone posed significant risk.

Richard was a salesperson at heart; a people person. He could maintain a composed appearance under any amount of pressure. Despite feeling overwhelmed with being scheduled to present to so many people, he knew he could keep it together. He was tired after spending most of the night putting the finishing touches on his slides, but he was up for the challenge.

About 15 minutes into Richard's two-hour presentation, he realized he was losing his audience. Watches and smart-phones were being checked, glances towards the exit became more frequent. One young gentleman in the front row sat forward and looked at the ground. All of this rattled the usually confident Richard, and he took steps to move through his slides at a faster clip.

By the time he reached the final slide he was about 20 minutes ahead of schedule. As he opened the floor to questions, his audience looked more like a group of money-conscious tourists following an overnight bus ride than Richard's future successors. Silence. The only movement came from the young guy at the front, finally raising his head to make eye contact with Richard. His "question" was a pointed statement, "I've been sitting here for two hours, and I don't know why. What's the point?" Richard's first reaction was jump to his own defense, but he caught himself, "I was hoping to illustrate the path that I took to get to this stage in my career. I was hoping to create a blueprint for the newer members of the team."

"Can I go now, please?"

"Sure."

With that, Mr. Head-down, who was quite tall when he was not looking at the floor, strode from the room. This was the cue for more of the audience to start rifling through bags and moving chairs. When things eventually calmed down, Richard's audience was reduced by half. He took questions and wrapped up after 10 minutes.

As he packed up his equipment, Richard reflected on how the presentation had gone. Not well, obviously. He imagined himself sitting in the audience and replayed some of the delivery. As he thought about the bullet points and his talk, it struck him. Unless his audience had been thoroughly briefed before joining the session, it would have been hard to follow the points. Richard's talk was based on the assumption that everyone knew why they were there. In the absence of this context, it was just collection of bullet points describing Richard's career in a linear fashion. And he'd subjected these poor individuals to two hours of this?

"DICK" SYNDROME

Richard—Dick—has a problem. It's a problem that most of us experience, and for the purposes of this explanation let's call it Dick Syndrome. Dick Syndrome describes the situation where you know a subject so well that you are terrible at teaching it. You know it so well that you do everything on autopilot, and so when you have to explain it to other people, they struggle to follow you.

Dick Syndrome affects all of us in different areas. It's not that we are bad at explaining things, it's just that we forget how much we had to learn and practice to get so good at a skill that we now do it without thinking. When we deliver presentations, like Richard, we are often talking about something that we know really well.

Dick Syndrome is easy to overcome, but it requires conscious thought. If we spend a little time to un-Dick our presentations, we are more likely to have happier audiences and an easier time presenting as a result.

Here's what to do to un-Dick your presentations:

1. Reflect on your audience;
2. Ask what they want to know;
3. Ask what they need to know; and
4. Ask where you want them to go.

REFLECT ON YOUR AUDIENCE

The main point of this exercise is to choose a destination for your presentation. To find out where you want your audience to go. What action do you want them to take? Before you do that, however, you have to think about where they are now. Create a quick draft of an audience profile: What is their area of expertise? Why are they attending your presentation? What is their level of knowledge around your subject matter?

WHAT DO THEY WANT TO KNOW

Ask yourself what your audience wants to know about your subject matter or items related to your subject matter. This could be gripes, wishes, or just items of interest. Brainstorm a quick list, and we'll use it later to help choose our destination.

WHAT DO THEY NEED TO KNOW

Identify what your audience needs to know. You will probably have a good idea already of the information you need to share with your audience, but it's worth making some notes now. The previous step will help you to understand the information they need.

WHERE DO YOU WANT THEM TO GO

Now, let's choose the destination for your presentation. The destination is where you want to end, or what action you want the audience to take as a result of your presentation. The type of audience you will have, coupled with what they want to know and what they need to know will help to drive you through your presentation to this final destination.

Make the decision about the destination now. Choosing now is important because it will give the focus to clearly lay out your presentation going forward. Look at this like a vacation. We're choosing where to go for vacation now so we can plan and pack. Not choosing the destination now is like packing your bags, driving to the airport, and thinking, "Where shall I go?"

PREPARATION CHECKLIST:

1. Know what your desired outcome is

5

KNOW YOUR STUFF

Dana Stevens was five minutes into her presentation, and things weren't going well. Despite only half of the anticipated audience present, a grand total of 10, Dana was still on edge. She couldn't remember anything. Every time she opened her mouth, a few shaky words would escape, and the audience grew more uncomfortable. She turned back towards her slides and looked for a prompt to remind her of the next part of her script that she'd forgotten.

Dana had been up all night going over her script. She'd written it a month ago and had practiced daily since then. The topic, human resource management best practices, was a new one for her, so she had left nothing to chance. She'd only transferred to the department six weeks ago, and her boss believed in trial by fire. She'd reviewed the script every spare moment that she got. Kids eating dinner, time for review. Husband washing dishes or watching TV, out came the presentation text. Train, bus, McDonald's drive-thru. Everywhere. Over and over and over again. Dana had been over the script so many times, she now hated the words.

Now, standing in front of her audience, none of those hated words would come. Nothing. Even more reason to hate them! The nerves had gotten the better of Dana. And the topic was so unfamiliar that Dana couldn't find enough wisdom to explain her bullet points. Now, she was only a third of the way through her talk, and she'd lost her audience. She wanted to curl up in a ball and forget all this had ever happened.

Have you ever been here? You've spent all night working on your speech. You've got your slides all laid out. Every heading and bullet point carefully worded to help you remember what to say at the right moment. You've practiced. You're confident that this will be okay. You are nervous as heck, but you are comfortable that you'll be able to get through it.

The time has almost come to get up on stage. Your heart's pumping faster and faster the closer it gets. You take some deep breaths and do a final check of your slides. Suddenly, you're feeling a little panicky that you might forget something. You review the bullets and run through your speech. You basically remember everything but you're less confident now, which makes you more panicky.

The time has come. They're calling your name. You take a big gulp of air, grab everything you need, and head out to the stage. You look out into the audience and begin to introduce yourself. You're suddenly overcome with a feeling of powerlessness as all those sets of eyes peer back. You flick on the slides and begin talking about the overall point of your presentation. You turn around, read the first bullet point, turn back to the audience and elaborate. Not as smooth as you'd practiced, but good enough. Point number two. The audience begin to shift uncomfortably. The panic returns. Point number three. Going okay. Next slide. Coughs from the audience. More panic from you. Then, tragedy strikes.

Slide number two, bullet point number one. You've gone blank. What were you meant to say about this? More panic. You wrack your mind. It's on the tip of your tongue, but the words just won't come. You feel the blood rush to your face.

You have a fuzzy idea of what you're meant to say, but you just can't remember the detail. This was so clear last night. It was clear a few minutes ago. Now, it's completely gone. You realize you haven't said anything for what feels like hours. "Sorry!" you say, and then look for something to do to help you remember. Then you realize, your notes! You apologize again and then check the laptop. Taking PowerPoint off projection mode, you quickly check the notes for the slide and then resume. Everything goes okay for the next two slides, then the same thing happens again. Halfway through your presentation, you're ready for a stiff drink or two.

This situation is common. We've become so accustomed to letting PowerPoint guide us and not having to be the expert on what we're talking about that this is a daily routine for a majority of companies. Presenters are unprepared or prepared in the wrong ways. This results in a massive amount of wasted time for all involved.

There are many differences between a good presentation delivery and a bad one. One of the key features of a bad presentation delivery is a slide deck full of bullet points and a presenter who does not have an in-depth understanding of the subject matter. The presenter is prepared. Very prepared. But the presenter has done the wrong preparation. The presenter has prepared to read and explain bullet points. The presenter has prepared to deliver words driven by a slide deck. The presenter has set themselves up to fail. They've created a presentation, which will be driven by slides, and expect to remember what to say for each of their carefully worded bullet points. Even if the presenter remembers everything perfectly, they fail by boring their audience to death through reading bullets. This is what you commonly hear termed "Death by PowerPoint." More accurately, this should be called "Death by person who doesn't know how to communicate and expects software to do the job for them."

POWERPOINT DOESN'T SUCK, YOU DO

A presentation is not about PowerPoint, or Keynote, or any other software solution. It is about communication.

The Oxford Dictionary defines a presentation as "a talk giving information about something." Somehow, though, we've managed to mangle presentation into meaning "an elaboration of bullet points on a projected document." Now, the long and the short of this is, you, your peers, your superiors and subordinates, can continue to deliver slide-driven, coma-inducing readings of slide decks. The trouble you will collectively face is diminished relevance within your organization as people start to wake up to the fact that their time is being wasted. Business people are getting more and more restless about attending sessions resembling reading time for kindergartners. And presenters that engage in the "read-elaborate", slide-driven style of delivery risk being switched off. Unable to communicate ideas clearly, their organizational influence reduces, negatively impacting their chances for advancement and special projects.

There is a simple solution to the "read-elaborate" style of presentation delivery. It's a solution that will free you up to do a more dynamic and authentic talk. It's a solution that is more credible and more likely to persuade. It's a solution that the average car salesman uses without even thinking of it as a technique.

KNOW YOUR STUFF

Here's what happens when you know your stuff.

You become more confident. When you understand your subject matter deeply, and therefore less likely to have to remember "lines", your confidence increases. When you focus on remembering the words you have to say, you put undue pressure on yourself. You start to focus on saying the right words rather than saying the right thing. Instead of talking about what you know, you talk about what you have rote-memorized. The margin for error massively increases because you are not being natural. When you really understand a concept, memory just happens. Instead of trying to recall it, your mind absorbs it properly. You can then spit it out again without having to think.

Your credibility increases dramatically. Put yourself in the position of the audience. Imagine watching Presenter A reading from some slides. Now, imagine watching Presenter B confidently talking about a subject he or she knows well. Which presenter are you likely to trust more? Presenter B, of course. Presenter B has instant credibility because you can tell he knows his stuff.

Your relationship with the audience improves. You're talking from memory now. You're talking about something you know deeply, which results in you being more focused on your listeners and less focused on trying to remember things. As the connection between you and the audience improves, they begin to trust you more, and you don't need to work as hard to persuade them.

You can get buy-in more easily. If you've ever had to introduce a new idea or process, you'll know how difficult it is to get your listeners to accept your ideas or recommendations. When you understand your topic, speak confidently and credibly, and have a good relationship with the audience, it suddenly becomes easier to get the audience to buy in to what you're "selling."

THE KEY

If knowing your stuff is the key to confidence, credibility, rapport, and persuasion, what do you need to do get there?

You need to prepare for your presentation much differently than you are used to. Now that you have an outcome in mind (from the previous step), you need to ensure that you know your subject matter well. Where you would normally sit down and start drafting out slides or typing up bullet points, you should instead focus on filling in your knowledge gaps. You have an outcome, so you know where the presentation needs to go, now it's time to make sure you know enough about your subject matter to get you and the audience there.

PREPARATION CHECKLIST:

1. Know what your desired outcome is; and

2. Understand your topic deeply.

6

BUILD YOUR MAP

This was a terrible idea.

Barry swallowed hard, took one step towards the podium, and froze. 300 sets of eyes peered at the stage. Awoken by the movement in the shadows behind the bright lights. Barry Foster looked down one last time at his notes.

How had his business partner, Jeff, considered, even for a split-second, that this was a good idea?

Barry had a strong aversion to speaking in public. So strong, he'd done everything in his power to make sure Jeff was fit and able to deliver this critical product development keynote.

Barry had made sure Jeff's secretary had booked him on an early flight back from New York, just in case there were delays. He'd called Jeff this morning to confirm he'd woken up in time to catch his flight. He hadn't counted on maintenance staff striking and blockading the airports. No more Jeff.

Barry had barely looked at the presentation content. Wasting time making sure Jeff could get back to do it. Even if he had a few hours, how would he ever remember these lines?

Barry thought about escaping. Scurrying away to the sanctuary of his quiet office. He looked behind him, preparing to run. There was Jeff's secretary motioning for him to hurry and up and get out on stage. Barry gulped. What a nightmare! He closed his eyes, took a deep breath, and timidly walked on to the stage.

Predictably, Barry's presentation went badly. Despite having a good understanding of the subject matter, Barry was lost for words. He'd had no time to memorize the words in the script and wasn't familiar with the layout of the slides. There were no standing ovations, no wolf whistles, and Barry spent the remainder of the afternoon locked in his office quietly draining the bar fridge.

Imagine being in the same position as Barry. You're familiar with the subject matter of the presentation but haven't been involved in the preparation. You don't know what's in the script, but you're suddenly asked to stand in and deliver. What are you going to do?

For most people, this is a nightmare scenario. The solution, however, gives us a blueprint to use in any presentation. A blueprint which builds on the previous preparation we've done and dispenses with the need to memorize lines.

Just think about it, a solution that doesn't require writing out or memorizing lines. What a time saver! Importantly, it's not just a time saver, it's a confidence and credibility booster.

You are going to create a map. A map of your presentation that will provide the visual reminders you need to confidently walk through your presentation. You may have heard about a memorization technique called the Roman Room. It's like a simplified version of that. Very simplified. Let's call it the Presentation Path.

The Presentation Path is a simple way to map out your presentation content, so you have a visual representation of your presentation, which is easy to lock into your memory. It is purposely not a linear representation to facilitate memorization, eliminate dependencies, and increase flexibility when you are on stage.

Before we look at the Presentation Path, there are two disclaimers that you need to consider. First, the Presentation Path relies on you having completed the first two steps in the preparation process correctly. If you have your desired outcome and a full understanding of your subject matter (or as full an understanding as is possible), then the Presentation Path will work for you. Second, the Presentation Path is a reliable tool for an everyday business presentation. I would advise against using the Presentation Path for a performance presentation. A performance presentation is a delivery such as a TED talk or a paid speaking engagement.

With that said, now let's take a look at the Presentation Path:

THE PRESENTATION PATH

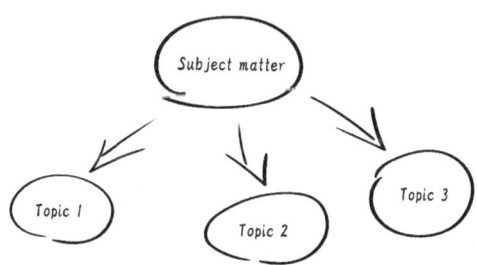

To keep it simple, the Presentation Path is split into two main areas: the subject matter bubble and the topic bubbles. The bubbles are joined together with a path.

The subject matter bubble represents the theme of the presentation. The theme can simply be the topic, but it is often helpful to use some kind of framing in the subject matter bubble. Framed positively, this core part of the Presentation Path can drive the atmosphere of your presentation.

Take for example, a presentation about a new time card system. You are the payroll manager and are implementing this new system effective Monday. Your subject matter bubble could read simply "New System" as a reminder about your presentation subject. Framed more positively, the bubble could contain the words "Save Time!" This is likely to drive the opening of your presentation differently. "New System" is likely to drive an introduction like, *"...Today, I'd like to introduce you to the new time card system..."* whereas "Save Time!" will drive a more positive framing, *"...Today, I'm going to introduce a system which will save you a significant amount of time each week..."*

Herman arrived at the office a little later than usual. He'd woken up late and had figured he'd make up time by catching a taxi. He didn't count on pre-election roadworks causing blockages to every major highway heading downtown. So, at 10.26am, Herman dropped his bag on the floor and quickly logged in to his desktop.

130 unread emails! After a weekend, this amount was normal, but this many emails coming in after 5pm on a weeknight was odd. He scanned through his inbox and saw the problem. Change requests! The user acceptance team were sending a crazy number of change requests. Closer inspection revealed many of them were duplicates of the same request sent by different members of the team. As Herman reviewed his emails, further change requests arrived in his mailbox. What a nightmare, he thought. It was company policy for him to act on every change request he receives. He was suddenly looking at a very long day. A day that started a little late would be ending very late.

Herman made a huge mistake. He was so sure of himself and his content that he was focused only on relaying the cold, hard facts. His aim was to get to the end of his presentation; to get it done. Herman didn't care about his audience, and it showed. He explained what he needed to, and he got through his presentation, but there are consequences for taking such a straight line. The consequences in Herman's case were quite obvious and severe. In a regular presentation, the "consequences" often take the form of resistance. When the presenter focuses solely on the fact-driven, straight line, the audience will generally resist in some form or another. In Herman's case, it was active resistance; in most cases, it will be passive. For example, taking no action following the presentation.

To avoid passive resistance, you need to focus on the audience. Remember that everything you do as presenter is for the audience. The audience are busy and they're doing you a favor by being there. You can return that favor by making your presentation audience-centric. The key to making your presentation audience-centric is to remember that you are the least important person in the room—the audience is all that matters.

To focus on your audience, you need to do the following:

1. Frame your presentation appropriately;

2. Display empathy;

3. Be interactive; and

4. Be conversational.

FRAME YOUR PRESENTATION

When confronted with the prospect of delivering a presentation, most people take the easy road. That is, they take what they think is going to be the easy road. It's uncomfortable to stand in front of an audience and talk, so they look for the most expedient way of doing their presentation. Unfortunately for them, what often happens is that the expediency happens during their preparation phase. The time saved during preparation often leads to more drawn out presentations, more bored audiences, and tougher questions. The icky-ness of presenting is reinforced, and the cycle repeats each time the person needs to deliver.

When you spend a little more time upfront, the likelihood is that your job will be much easier when you are on stage. To make your presentation easier, the time spent upfront should be focused on framing your presentation in a way that the audience can see how they benefit. When you deliver a benefit-driven presentation, as distinct from a purely logical A+B=C presentation, your audience will be more engaged, more receptive, more friendly, and more likely to retain information. All of this makes your job as a presenter easier.

To frame your presentation in the easiest way possible, take your core, bland subject matter, frame it for the audience, and open with that framed subject matter.

For example:

Bland subject: New computer system for customer tracking.

Framed subject: Save time on administrative tasks.

Opening: *"Today, I'll show you how to free-up 3 hours a week from your boring admin work."*

Bland subject: Compliance rules awareness.

Framed subject: Improved customer service through protecting customer information.

Opening: *"I've got good news for you. You can now improve your customer service and not have to work any harder! Give me just 10 minutes, and I'll show you how."*

Bland subject: End of year review and new year kick-off meeting.

Framed subject: Bonuses next year from productivity and revenue increases.

Opening: *"I'd like to talk about this year's poor company results, which will drive changes for next year and put more money in your pocket."*

Bland subject: Revised organization structure.

Framed subject: Improved line reporting.

Opening: *"From today, you'll get the answers you need when you need them."*

Bland subject: Project status update.

Framed subject: Improvements to the office.

Opening: *"You're just 4 weeks away from having more desk space and a faster computer."*

Bland subject: Overtime must be pre-approved before working or no pay.

Framed subject: Improving your work/life balance.

Opening: *"I'm going to reduce your working time and keep you from having to do un-necessary overtime."*

DISPLAY EMPATHY

If you can't connect with your audience, it is almost impossible to do an audience-centric presentation. It's very hard to connect with your audience if you can't empathize with them. Empathy is the ability to understand and share others' feelings. Herman's presentation wasn't very empathetic and, therefore, not successful. Had Herman shown more empathy for his audience, especially during question time, he would have been more likely to achieve better results.

Here's what you need to do. Think about the presentation from the audience's perspective. If you are talking about a change which will affect your audience, for example, new compliance processes or increased workload, you'll want to consider how they will likely feel before you get on stage. Get on stage and say words to the effect of, "...that's just how it is, deal with it", you're unlikely to score any points or listeners. This goes for your delivery and for your question handling session. You're also more likely to encounter passive resistance following your presentation. If, however, you explain the extra workload situation, listen to and understand the audience's concerns, and show the audience the best way forward, you'll do much better.

Herman took the "deal with it" approach in his presentation. An empathetic approach would have seen him show his understanding of audience concerns, acknowledgement of the fact that extra clicking was a problem for users, a sober explanation of why this situation currently exists, and perhaps a promise to investigate if changes are possible. Herman could also assure them by explaining that if the testers have any concerns while using the system, they should file a change request, and Herman will do his utmost to meet their needs. The audience will, at the very least, feel that Herman has listened to them and understood their concerns. Herman is much less likely to have received those 100+ emails.

BE INTERACTIVE AND CONVERSATIONAL

An amazing thing happens when you interact with people. They pay attention to what you say! Conversely, lecturing people gives them little incentive to pay attention.

As a presenter, you want the audience to pay close attention and buy in to your proposals, so you need to focus on a delivery style that will engage them and leave them open to new ideas.

INTERACT

You interact with your audience by asking them questions. These questions can be regular or rhetorical (don't require an answer). By asking questions you build a closer bond with your audience as they feel that you are talking "with" them, rather than "at" them. You get your audience to pay closer attention because the rising tone of a question makes people sit up and listen.

To make questions effective, build empathy into the questions you ask. You might open your presentation with a question which sets the tone for an improved process to be implemented. The opening question could go something like this: "*Who else here is frustrated with the current ... process?*" The empathy is built in to this question because it supposes you already understand that people are frustrated with said process.

Use rhetorical questions to make attention grabbing transitions between the topics you talk about. Transition between talking about flat sales to recovery plan with something like: "*What are we going to do to improve sales? Well, let me introduce you to our recovery plan...*"

CONVERSE

Increase the audience-centricity of your delivery, and build great rapport with your audience by talking to them as you would in regular conversation: naturally. Don't make the mistake of a million amateur presenters by thinking that because you're delivering a formal presentation, your tone must be formal and robotic.

Audiences connect with, and trust people, who they see as honest. You intrinsically appear more honest if you speak naturally. If you speak from a semi-practiced script, speaking quite robotically, the audience is going to trust you less. You look like you might be hiding something (even if all you're hiding is your lack of understanding of the subject matter).

Speak naturally, conversationally, and build a trusting relationship with your audience. If you've followed the steps in this book so far to prepare your presentation, you should be in good shape at this point to deliver your talk with a conversational tone.

PREPARATION CHECKLIST:

1. Know what your desired outcome is;

2. Understand your topic deeply;

3. Draft your Presentation Path; and

4. Understand your audience and how to talk to them.

8

FIRST REHEARSAL

S tella Harris had been here before.
Project management was a struggle at the best of times. A constant balancing act between innovation and managing expectations of what was actually possible. Today was one of those days. This afternoon, Stella was due to give a presentation on the progress of her biggest project to the project stakeholders.

These types of presentations never went well. A room full of tired business people who cared little about the details, impatient to hear results. Rarely had Stella done one of these presentations and left the room feeling she had accomplished something. Each time she completed a talk, she walked away knowing the stakeholders had absorbed nothing. An exercise in ceremony.

She was determined today would be different. No more blank looks. No more tapping feet. No more sleeping stake-holders. Today, she would do her presentation differently. Dispense with the bullet points and focus on delivering an audience-focused talk to highlight the great strides made so far, and to manage expectations about the potential obstacles to come.

Having done so many of these presentations, Stella knew that reading slide after slide of bullet points to her audience was not going to work. Today she would focus on delivering the information she knew they wanted to hear and gently slide in the request for additional budget at the end of her talk when she had them primed. She knew her project well and so set about drafting the main points she would speak on, four in total.

In under 30 minutes, Stella had the basis of her presentation. A simple diagram showing her subject and the four supporting points she would talk about. Next, she launched PowerPoint and started building her slide deck. Again, she didn't want to overwhelm her audience with bullet points, so her focus was very much on making her slides visual.

Stella decided she would have her slides act as support for each point she talked about. Thus, she located four high quality images, each one representative of the four points she would talk about in her presentation. She added a title slide and a closing slide to bookend the images, and she was ready to go.

Time was getting on, so Stella saved her work and stepped out for lunch, confident she was going to deliver a great presentation. Finally, she would deliver a talk that kept her stakeholders interested and drove them to action. To celebrate, Stella took lunch at a new Italian place next door to her office.

Stella's presentation came and went. It was received as her previous presentations had been. The audience non-plussed; lolling around, uninterested for the bulk of the talk; and resistant to calls for extra budget at the end. The difference this time was the outright complaints about not having bullet points to review afterwards. If there were no handouts with bullet points for later review, how could they possibly understand her presentation?

What happened? Stella had planned well. She prepared visual slides, so the audience could focus on listening to her. Her delivery was weighted towards saying things she knew her audience wanted to hear. But the audience didn't care. Her stakeholders seemed to be in the audience out of duty and hadn't listened to her. They wanted a summary of the presentation in the form of the usual bullet points, so they could read about what they hadn't listened to later on.

Stella had two problems. First, the audience did what they normally do. They are so used to going to dead-boring presentations that they attend on autopilot. Literally, they are programmed to not pay attention and use the slides (printed or email) to review what happened while they were daydreaming. Second, she missed part of her preparation. She did most things right, but she hit her PowerPoint slides too early. Stella should have rehearsed before she jumped to PowerPoint. Only through rehearsing first will she be able to find holes in her presentation and fill those gaps.

A slide deck is only effective when it comes after we know what we're going to say and how we're going to say it. When it comes at this stage, it will naturally support and improve our talk. Stella should have rehearsed her talk and become confident speaking without slides first. It's when you are confident speaking without slides that the introduction of slides will improve your delivery.

Take talk shows, where the host does their monologue and slides appear over their right shoulder as they talk. The monologue is engaging, often humorous, because we are focused on the presenter and the words they are saying. We don't need the visuals to be engaged by their speech. Because we are so engaged by their speech, however, when visuals are used to complement the monologue they have additional impact which engages us further. The point of all this is that the talk show needs to know what they are going to say in order to deliver an amazing talk... And you should too.

Here's how to rehearse your presentation without slides:

1. Visualize your presentation path;

2. Stand up;

3. Maintain an open body position;

4. Don't stop; and

5. Record, review, adjust.

VISUALIZE YOUR PRESENTATION PATH

The key to delivering a natural sounding presentation is not to follow a script but to speak about what you know. In the previous steps, you have ensured a deep understanding of your subject matter, and you planned out what points you need to talk about. So, to rehearse effectively, you need to commit the Presentation Path you created to memory.

Memorizing your Presentation Path should be relatively easy, especially if the bubbles you created are labelled with only one or two keywords. If you struggle to memorize the Presentation Path, fear not. I have a solution for you to help you commit it to memory. The key is to think in images.

It is much easier for your brain to process and remember images. So, instead of trying to remember your keywords, swap them out for images. Imagine your talk is about the new marketing campaign your firm will employ due to the bad sales results you have had over the last year. Perhaps the supporting points in your Presentation Path are laid out like this:

1. Review of bad sales results;

2. New marketing campaign; and

3. Forecast sales for next year.

The keywords in your Presentation Path might be like this:

1. REVIEW;

2. CAMPAIGN; and

3. COMING UP.

You could also use a vivid image to remember each of the points:

1. Review of the bad sales results: Imagine a big zero dropping on your boss's head and your boss crying as a result;

2. New marketing campaign: Imagine someone from the marketing department wiping your boss's tears away with a "new" handkerchief; and

3. Forecast sales for next year: Imagine your boss skipping happily amongst busy sales people while he throws dollar bills around.

Once you can comfortably recall your entire Presentation Path, you are ready to continue with your rehearsal.

STAND UP

There is only one way to practice your presentation effectively, and that's in a standing position. When you stand up, you block out distractions around you. When you stand up, you gain a stronger focus on your presentation that's not available to you when you are seated.

David McGimpsey

One of the aims of practicing is to increase the fluidity with which you speak and the ease with which you can recall what you are saying. When you stand up, something happens that clears your mind, makes recall simpler, increases your confidence, and makes your speech smoother.

MAINTAIN AN OPEN BODY POSITION

As someone who has done thousands of presentations and coached thousands of others to do them, there is one thing above all else that instantly impresses the audience and builds your confidence and credibility. It has nothing to do with your content and has everything to do with the way we naturally judge people when we first meet them: Your visual communication.

Your visual communication tells the audience so much about you before you even open your mouth. It's therefore important that your visual communication appears natural and confident. Keeping it natural and confident means those first critical split-seconds give you a strong chance of being judged well.

This doesn't mean that you should practice your gestures as you rehearse. Practiced gestures never look good and will have the opposite effect of making you look natural and confident. Instead, you should practice, allowing yourself to be natural. If this sounds a bit weird, bear with me.

You already naturally use gestures and body language with confidence without being conscious about it. That's because it's natural! When you meet your friend in the shopping mall and you are chatting to them about your day, you gesture naturally. You don't think about it, but you do it. Imagine telling your friend about the hard day you've had; working at home, cleaning up, preparing the kids for school, then running them to baseball practice afterwards. As you are talking about all these things, your gestures just happen. Often you gesture in segments, breaking down tasks or time. The point is that you don't practice. Imagine telling your friend about your hard day with gestures that you had practiced earlier. It would look ridiculous! You'd have to pick particular words and link a gesture to those words. Not only would you have to remember what to say, you'd have to remember how to gesture when you say the word. Your speech becomes more stilted, your gestures robotic. Forgive your friend if they start to back away slowly.

So, how to gesture naturally? Maintain an open body position while you rehearse. No arm-folding, no hands behind your back, no hands clasped in front of you. Don't think about gestures, and don't worry if they don't happen automatically. The more you practice, the more clear you become about what you will say, and more natural the gestures will be.

DON'T STOP

When you make a mistake, it can be tempting to get frustrated and want to start again from the beginning of your speech. Don't do it! By starting again, you are training yourself into a mindset which does not tolerate mistakes. To be a truly good presenter, you have to be able to roll with the mistakes and keep moving forward. Granted, at the outset of your rehearsals you're going to make a lot of mistakes, but just remain confident and continue to the end. You will improve with time.

If time runs out for rehearsal and you are still making some mistakes, don't worry. Every presenter makes mistakes. How they handle those mistakes is key. When a mistake is made, don't let it become the focus. Correct it and move on. The audience won't notice, and even if they do, they won't care.

RECORD, REVIEW, ADJUST

Time permitting, record and review your rehearsals. Get out your smartphone, tablet, or video camera, and have it running while you practice. After you've finished an entire delivery watch it back. It can be tough to watch yourself, but you'll get over that feeling quickly.

Reviewing your rehearsal is extremely valuable. Often what you think you are doing badly, you'll discover, is not bad at all, which can help you relax. You will also pick up things that are not so good that you'll want to work to change. For instance, a constantly tapping foot. During your review, pick one or two things you want to work on improving and focus on them during your next rehearsal. Rehearse, record, review, and adjust as often as you need to.

PREPARATION CHECKLIST:

1. Know what your desired outcome is;

2. Understand your topic deeply;

3. Draft your Presentation Path;

4. Understand your audience and how to talk to them; and

5. Rehearse.

9

SLIDES

Here's the sucky thing about slides. Most people see them as necessary in presentations. People see them as so important that the word "presentation" is often used by them to mean "slide deck". With slides seen as a requirement, often the main event, the slide deck becomes the star of the show. Event and meeting organizers request the slide deck in advance of the day so they can judge what you're going to say in your presentation. Needless to say, all of this is nonsense and placing too much emphasis on what will usually end up as nothing more than a prompting device.

THE KEYS TO A GOOD SLIDE DESIGN

There are several keys to good slide design:

1. Know what you are going to say and create your slides at the end of the preparation process (you're reading this book so you should already "get" this one);

2. Use slides for impact rather than information;

3. Cut slides that don't enhance what you say; and

4. Slides should not be reading/handout material.

CREATE YOUR SLIDES AT THE END OF THE PREPARATION PROCESS

For further information, see the book you are currently reading :)

USE SLIDES FOR IMPACT RATHER THAN INFORMATION

Lesley Robinson is standing in front of her audience. She's shaking a little but manages to hold herself together. She flicks on the slides to reveal three bullet points outlining what she will talk about in her presentation. She explains each point to her audience. She will talk about the bad sales figures her department achieved two years ago; the changes put in place a year ago to combat the decline; and the stellar results that have been achieved in the last year.

Lesley proceeds to walk her audience through her first two points, aided by more bullety slides before turning to the most exciting news. She's almost trembling with excitement to reveal the results that have been achieved.

As Lesley transitions to her last point, the great results, she flicks the slides over to a chart showing a short but massive upswing in sales in the last 12 months. Aided by the heading on the graph, Lesley begins to explain the bad situation of the past. "For many years, our sales were flat," she says motioning a line movement alongside the chart, "Then, two years ago, we really hit a wall. Sales dropped off a cliff." More hand gestures, this time pointing downwards.

"We made some changes to how sales reps explain our products a year ago. We also changed the pricing structure a little to give us the flexibility to offer free trials." A smile began forming on Lesley's face. "As a result," she moved with a flourish to right side of the chart, "we have increased sales by 300% over the last year!"

Lesley looked expectantly into the audience. She wasn't sure what feedback she would get, but such a fantastic result warranted something. Not fireworks or champagne, but a round of applause or some positive comments at least. Maybe, some questions?

Nothing. Silence. Crickets.

Here's the problem. When Lesley wasn't boring her audience to death with bullet points, she was trying to impact them with information they already knew. At the point when Lesley said "...300% over the last year!" the audience had already been looking at that upswing in the chart for 5 minutes. Lesley had a double-whammy. Her slides were boring and contained nothing impactful.

Here's a way for Lesley to instantly impact her audience: Split her one-slide chart into two slides. Instead of showing the entire chart at once, she could instead show the first half of the chart with the years and flat sales and sudden drop. The second slide can contain the full chart including the 300% upswing. After creating both of these slides, the impact comes down simply to timing. She should show the second slide (full chart) at the point that she says "...300% over the last year!" Doing this will have much more impact because a) Lesley doesn't give the game away before she talks about it, and b) the slide change at the point where Lesley wants to impact the audience will catch their attention.

CUT SLIDES THAT DON'T ENHANCE WHAT YOU SAY

Don't include slides in your presentation for additional information. If the audience requires take-away reading material, prepare separate handouts that you can distribute at the time of your choosing. Don't include backup slides in case you forget your speech. Don't include any slide that doesn't act as an impactful background support to what you're saying.

SLIDES SHOULD NOT BE READING/HANDOUT MATERIAL

If you are presenting a complex topic and your audience need further reading, prepare some additional handouts for them. Don't fall into the trap of using the slides as content that can double as handout material. Doing this will create a situation where your slides contain so much detail that your audience will read during your presentation and not listen to you. Create separate handouts in a different document and distribute it at the end of your presentation.

SLIDE DESIGN GUIDELINES

TEXT

If it's not clear already, then this book is obviously not the ranty work I had set out to create: Text should be minimized, even eradicated, on your slides. Text promotes reading and therefore promotes not listening, so be very selective about what you write on your slides.

What I find a good rule of thumb is any text should be immediately relevant as soon as it appears. If it does not follow this rule, then it is a distraction.

BULLET POINTS

Bullet points are appropriate for so many different things. They are fantastic at listing product benefits in sales letters. They are amazing at recording minutes in meetings. They are a great way to quickly organize simple data into a readable format.

What bullets are not good at is being a presentation tool. In a presentation, bullet points become a distraction, forcing the audience to read the important list that you're displaying on your slide, obviously because you want the audience to read them, right?

It's important to realize that bullets come with baggage. Every presentation that anyone has ever attended has used bullet points. Usually too many bullet points, usually in too small a font. Usually badly constructed. The idea is that most bullet points simply get read out to the audience by the presenter. So, when a member of your audience sees a bullet point in your presentation, irrespective of how it's presented, it comes with the baggage of enduring a billion bad past presentations.

Before adding bullet points to your slide, consider why you are using them. Is it just because it's the default functionality, default template, in PowerPoint or Keynote? Remember that no work of art was ever created by using a template.

FONTS

Your font selection is crucial. It can mean the difference between professional looking sides and a pile of amateur garbage. Luckily there are only a few simple rules you need to follow.

Choose a sans serif font for your slides.

To understand what a sans serif font is, you first need to understand a serif font. A serif is like a tail or an extremity on a font. Little lines and dots that add emphasis to the font. Fonts that use serifs are Times New Roman, Century, and Georgia. This book uses a serif font for the content. In a book, using a serif font increases the readability. When projected, however, a serif font can reduce readability and look quite messy. A sans serif font is one without serifs. These are fonts like Arial, Helvetica, and Verdana. Using a sans serif font in your slides will make the projected slide look sharper and cleaner.

Stick with the same font throughout.

Don't play designer when you're building your slide deck and mess around with different combinations of fonts. Stick with the one sans serif font you chose throughout. If you want to emphasize something or create a heading, do so using bold or by increasing the size of the font. Try to maintain consistency from one slide to the other with what sizes, styles, and colors you use for emphasis, header, and body text.

Choose appropriate sizes.

There are no particular sizes that are better, as each font is different, but there are some guidelines that you can follow.

Use sizes that can be read at a distance. If the font can't be seen from the back of the room, it's too small. Conversely, avoid sizes that bleed into each other. If the text is halfway into your pie chart the font is probably too big.

HEADINGS

Despite the defaults you might find in PowerPoint and Keynote templates, I caution against using headlines for every slide. Having a headline on a slide reduces the impact of the slide because when you flick over the audience will automatically read the heading before looking at anything else. If you want them to be impacted by a number when you flick on the slide, make the number the focus of the slide. If you have an image you want the audience to pay attention to, show them the image and don't distract with a headline explaining the image.

LABELS

Don't make the common mistake of labeling everything on your slides. This is a graph. This is line. This is a dip in the graph (worst ever). This is the massive spike in sales we are talking about.

Labeling everything is a waste of time and will burn out your audience's eyeballs. They don't need to have everything labeled in such a detailed way—that's what your voice is for. Next time you feel like adding a label to something, stop and consider if it would be more effective to rattle your vocal chords and label the thing with your voice. If the answer is "yes", then do it. If the answer is "no", then why were you going to label it?

WHITESPACE

This is perhaps the most important part of your slide design. What you don't put on your slides is more important than what you do. Each of your slides should be made up mostly of whitespace (if you are not using a white background, think of whitespace as open/blank space). The less information you have on each slide, the more impact the information on the slide has. The more information you have on a particular slide, the more the audience has to think about where to look and what each slide element means. Maximize whitespace and minimize audience confusion.

Note: If you fill an entire slide with a text-free image and no additional elements, the whitespace rule doesn't apply.

COLOR

Minimize the amount of color used. Pick a color for the background and stick with it. Pick a font color and stick with it. Only change the font color when you need to strongly emphasize or de-emphasize what's written.

IMPACT

If your slides add no impact to your presentation, then they are a waste of time. You are better off sending handouts or a report to your audience before or after your talk. Remember that walking your audience through the bullet points on your slides is just the same as walking them through the bullet points on a handout that everyone is looking at (except the latter is not as shiny-bright).

What "impact" here means is to emphasize something to your audience through visuals and timing. If I show you 5 bullet points and read through them with you, you know what's coming and there is no impact. In this case, the slides are wasted because they add nothing. In fact, they detract from the talk because the presenter is reading from the slides.

On the other hand, imagine I'm presenting about the new cost-saving measures we instituted at our company a couple months back. As I say, "*...and we're now spending a whopping 50% less per month on consumables...*", I flip to a slide showing 50% and a down arrow. Now, that has impact. No one knew what I was going to say until I said it, and the slide showed up just in time to reinforce what I was saying. This is what handouts and bullet points can't do.

IMAGES AND CLIPART

Avoid clipart, and make use of high quality images. Sites such as iStockPhoto.com and DepositPhotos.com have searchable databases and are great places to get your hands on relevant stock images for your slides.

How you use images is as important as which ones you use. Images tend to be used as decoration for bullet points or slabs of text. Typically, you'll see slides with a block of text on the left and a related image on the right. Instead of doing this, think differently. Images are better used to enhance what you're saying. Think about a talk show monologue. When the host does their bit, the images flash to the side of the host to enhance what is being said at that moment.

ANIMATIONS

Aim to avoid animations in your deck. Here's why: Animations are distracting. While you have text and objects bouncing around the screen, the audience is paying less attention to what you're actually saying. A good rule of thumb is that the audience should be able to look at your slide and instantly get the message. Animation gets in the way of understanding quickly what's being said.

GRAPHS AND CHARTS

Not everything should be equal. When creating graphs and charts, design them to put emphasis on the important data. If I'm an audience member and you show me a graph, I want to get the point, quickly. I want to listen to you, and I want to see the key graphic information without having to turn my attention away from you, the presenter. Show the key information on graphs and charts by enlarging the key information and reducing the size of the rest. Once you've designed a chart, step back and look at the slide. If someone handed you this chart, could you find the key information without prompting? No? Back to the drawing board then.

TABLES

Like charts, not everything in a table should be equal. Highlight the key data in a table with different colors or different sizes. Avoid making your audience search for the key point or they will stop listening to you.

EMPHASIZE WHAT YOU'RE TALKING ABOUT

Remember how the slides are there to support you? Well, that means that when you say something important, the slides should help emphasize that thing. If you're talking about the mid-year financial downturn, the relevant number is the drop. Displaying a graph for the full year might show the drop pictorially but doesn't really emphasize it.

A good way to emphasize something is to make it standout. If you have a pie chart, make the important segment stick out. If you have a bar chart and want to emphasize one bar, make the color contrast with all the other bars. If you have a month of sales numbers in a table and want to emphasize one of the numbers, make the unimportant numbers small and gray, make the important number big. Color the important number black or red.

POINTING

Have you ever sat in the audience of a presentation and watched the back of the speaker's head while they point to a section of the slide with their hand or laser? Have you watched that red laser circling around the text or section of graph and felt like you were wasting your time? Have you looked at all the other information on the slide and wondered what else needs to be pointed at before this nightmare is over? If you answered yes to any or all of these questions, you belong to the silent majority of audience members the world over.

Pointing to your slides is a definite no-no if you are doing a goal-driven presentation. It's a no-no because it bores the audience. It also takes their focus away from you, and it becomes more difficult to get that focus back. The biggest reason this is a no-no, however, is that it sheds clear light on a fundamental issue with your slide design: You have too much information on the slide you are pointing at. Look at it this way, you're pointing at your slide because listening to your talk is not enough for the audience to understand what part of the slide you are referring to.

What does all this mean? Simplify your slides and... Stop pointing! Instead of using a laser, or your hand, start using a different pointing device: your voice. Instead of pointing with your hand at row 2 column 2 in the table, say, "As you can see from the bottom-right cell in the table, we're in trouble with our sales."

PREPARATION CHECKLIST:

1. Know what your desired outcome is;

2. Understand your topic deeply;

3. Draft your Presentation Path;

4. Understand your audience and how to talk to them;

5. Rehearse; and

6. Slides Ready

10

DRESS REHEARSAL

Perry Winter had done everything right. He'd ticked all the boxes. He knew where his audience needed to go. He knew detailed information about each one of them, their likes, dislikes, business frustrations. He knew his subject so well he could run rings around anyone else who tried to explain it. Perry was ready.

Despite being the middle of summer, it was raining hard today and Perry didn't have an umbrella. Luckily his customer's office was directly above the subway station. He left the subway and sprinted across the road to the lobby of the recently completed Cavill Tower office complex.

As he rode the elevator to the 47th floor, Perry checked off his preparation: Outcome, check! Subject matter, check! Audience knowledge, check! Presentation plan, check! Practice sessions, check! Slides, check! Good to go! There was a muted ding, the doors opened, and Perry strode confidently into the reception of Masterson Venture Capital.

Twenty minutes later, 2 minutes into his presentation, Perry's confidence had all but vanished. Despite all his preparation, all his practice, all his confidence, he was now floundering around like a drunk with thimbles on all fingers trying to sew a quilt. The pressure from Perry's need to secure crucial investment capital was only making things worse.

Things started badly from the get-go. Concerned about beginning on the correct slide, and that the advance button was working correctly, Perry's talk started choppy. He would say a few words and glance around at the slides to make sure the visual aids were lining up with his speech. He would later put this down to nerves given he could have checked the laptop's screen in front of him, which was in charge of projecting the slides.

The choppier Perry's talk became, the more the executives looked distracted and shifted uncomfortably in their seats. The more the executives looked uncomfortable, the more confidence Perry lost. The discomfort-doubt snowball continued to gain momentum until the head executive finally stood, "I think we've seen enough for today. You need to come back when you can talk to us more clearly." Perry tried to regain his composure, but he was done. The executives started to file out of the room while a secretary approached and helped Perry pack up.

Dazed and confused, the elevator ride was over in an instant. Other passengers shoved past Perry on their way out. What had happened? Of course, he knew. He had been confident about everything. He was confident about his subject, his audience, what to say and when to say it. He made some great slides. Not too much information, just enough. There was only one thing he was missing, one thing that had tripped him up. He wasn't confident about the synchronization between his talk and his slides. He stuttered, stammered, checked, double-checked, and triple-checked. By then, he'd lost his audience.

Perry's biggest problem now was what his business partners were going to say.

Perry had just experienced a problem common to presenters trying the goal-driven style of presentation for the first time. He did everything right. He followed a preparation process almost identical to that outlined in this book. He missed one small step, however, and that threw out his presentation. He missed a vital unification step. He skipped the dress rehearsal.

Throughout your presentation preparation, you have been focused on your audience and your delivery. You didn't worry about your slides until the very end of the process. This is great and will make for a fantastic delivery, but only if you do a dress rehearsal. The dress rehearsal brings together your delivery and slides. It synchronizes them so that the slides have the desired effect on your delivery: support and impact.

In the dress rehearsal, you need to do exactly the same as the previous rehearsal stage, just with the addition of slides. During this rehearsal, it is important to look in the direction of the audience throughout your delivery, that is, make efforts to avoid looking back at the projector screen to check which slide you are up to. To help with this goal, try positioning your laptop computer so the screen is visible in front of you. You should be able to see it when you are looking at your audience, so you can always check what is being projected behind you while you look forward.

Practice as many times as you can to become comfortable till your presentation and slides are unified. If you have time to record, review, and adjust, all the better.

A final note on your dress rehearsal: If you will not have time to do a dress rehearsal, it will most likely be better for your delivery to skip the slides. Adding slides without the opportunity to do a dress rehearsal can destroy an awesome presentation.

David McGimpsey

PREPARATION CHECKLIST:

1. Know what your desired outcome is;

2. Understand your topic deeply;

3. Draft your Presentation Path;

4. Understand your audience and how to talk to them;

5. Rehearse;

6. Slides ready; and

7. Dress rehearsal.

PART THREE

11

Bringing it all together

In this final chapter, let's review everything we've covered so far about the goal-driven approach to presentations and then put it into practice with some business scenarios.

REVIEW

1. Choose your destination
a.k.a. Decide an outcome.

Decide where your audience needs to go. This should be your first step. When you choose the outcome you need, your subsequent planning will be clearer and easier.

Example outcome: Audience understands that they should check that they can login to the new system.

Example outcome: Audience accepts policy change and demonstrates their understanding through asking questions.

2. Know your stuff
a.k.a. Become a subject matter expert.

When you're a subject matter expert, you can talk about your material naturally and confidently. You're more prepared to stand in front of an audience and talk about your material than someone who has prepared for days but doesn't know the subject as deeply. If something you wanted to talk about slips your mind, you don't get hot and bothered. Instead, you just continue on with the next point. Contrast this with the ultra-prepared presenter who doesn't know their subject deeply. If the presenter forgets a line in their script, it can spell the end of the presentation by throwing the speaker into a downward spiral of "umms", "ahhs", and apologies.

Bottom line? Know your subject inside out.

3. Build your map
a.k.a. Draft a Presentation Path.

Now it's time to put your outcome and subject matter knowledge together and draft a Presentation Path. The Presentation Path takes the place of a script. It is designed to be easily memorized to help you be as natural and confident as possible when you're on stage.

Your Presentation Path will consist of a number of bubbles. One central bubble contains the subject matter or central theme of your presentation. The remaining, surrounding bubbles contain the topics, or points, which you will talk about that lead to your desired outcome.

It is important to represent the content of the bubbles with short keywords or an image to make memorization and recall simpler.

4. EVERYTHING YOU DO IS FOR THEM
a.k.a. Frame your presentation for the audience.

Your desired outcome most likely requires the audience to take some kind of action. Perhaps it's simply to see your point of view or buy-in to a project. Maybe it's a more complex decision, like buying your product or signing up for a course. Whatever it is, you need to frame everything you say with the audience in mind.

The most important thing here is to empathize with your audience. Think about your subject matter. Is it going to help the audience solve a particular problem? Frame your presentation around this. Explain to the audience that you feel their pain. You know what it's like to suffer through the problems they're going through. And you have a solution! On the other hand, if the subject matter is likely to inconvenience the audience (changed rules they need to follow), consider how the inconvenience they will experience now can help the audience in the future. You might be telling them they need to complete an extra report at the end of each week, but the bonus might be that they don't have to sit through those long weekly status update meetings anymore.

Think about how you will talk about your subject matter through the framed lens you have identified.

5. FIRST REHEARSAL
a.k.a. First practice.

Using your deep knowledge of the subject matter and your memorized Presentation Path, stand up and rehearse your presentation. Practice all the way to the end of your talk. Try to avoid restarting if you make an error so you get into the habit of treating mistakes as something to quickly recover from.

Your practice is best done when you are video recording, so you can playback and review your performance. If you can't record, at the very least, try to practice in front of a mirror.

6. SLIDES
a.k.a. Build your slides.

Now that you know what you are going to say, you know what parts of your talk are best supported or emphasized. This is what your slides are for: support and emphasis. If you have a slide that doesn't emphasize something you are saying or doesn't support you, cut it.

Here is a quick checklist of what to do or not to do with your slide design:

- Ideally, cut out your bullet points;

- Minimize text;

- Use sans serif fonts (eg. Arial, Helvetica, Tahoma);

- Stick with one font (use different sizes and bold to differentiate regular text and headings);

- Use high quality images where appropriate;

- Enhance slides with whitespace;

- If something needs a label, there's probably something too complicated about your slide design;

- Emphasize the important points in charts and tables;

- De-emphasize the unimportant details in charts and tables;

- Avoid animations;

- Time the change of slides, or reveal of information, with what you say for maximum impact; and

- Don't create slides you need to point at (if you need to point, your slides are driving rather than supporting).

7. DRESS REHEARSAL
a.k.a. Practice with slides.

Time to practice again. This time with your slides. The point of this round of rehearsals is to unify your talk with the timing and display of your slides.

Practice delivering your speech and making the slides appear at the appropriate time to maximize the impact of both the slide and the words you are saying. All the time try to avoid looking back at the slides behind you (or to the side of you) as this will diminish their impact and take the audience's focus away from you and place it on the slide.

CASE STUDY

Howard has worked in the marketing department at Intatech for over 21 years. In his time there, he had never seen demands placed on the team like they'd experienced in the last six months. In that short span of time, they'd been asked, by the company president, to create and test some complicated offers.

The firm's sales weren't bad, but they'd been flat for the last few quarters. At their summer retreat, the company executives had hatched an idea to offer discount offers on products. They would lure back previously loyal customers who had, at one point other, discovered deeper discounts with the competition and gradually disappeared. Once recaptured, these customers would be encouraged to stay put using a mixture of an exclusivity contract and yearly bonus discounts.

These new offers sounded wonderful to everyone at the company, except those who would be involved in the implementation. Designing the process and overseeing the project fell to Howard and the marketing team.

The program seemed simple at first. Create some new contracts and offer codes, and set the salespeople lose. As with most things, the devil was in the details. These offers would only be available to corporate customers who used to buy from Intatech but now shopped elsewhere. The offer codes and discounts applied would vary based on which competitor was currently being used. The contract terms would vary based on the offer codes. All this had to be operated and tracked automatically to ensure that the sales reps didn't get tied up with admin work when they could be selling. All this added up to a major headache for Howard and his team.

After a long six months, hundreds of hours of overtime, enough coffee to power a jet engine, an office meltdown, three public arguments, and some disciplinary action, the program was operational. Howard was a walking zombie, as were most of his team, but they had done it. And the program had had the desired impact. Sales were amazing! Customers were returning. Salespeople were hitting bonus again. Everyone was happy. Except Howard.

Howard had one final thing to do before he wrapped the project up. A presentation. The whole company was waiting to hear about the miracle Howard and his team had pulled off. Howard was jittery about delivering his presentation, but it was good for his career. The project had been a success at a firm that had settled for mediocrity in the past few years. Howard could show some of the obstacles he'd overcome, the battles he'd fought and won with what he termed "hard diplomacy", and how he'd united his team to pull Intatech out of the funk.

Howard had chosen the goal-driven approach for his presentation.

ESSENTIAL DATA

Presenter: Howard Flint.

Subject: Project implementation and results.

Audience: Intatech managers and staff (approximately 300 attendees).

Timing: Friday, 4pm.

Room: Large auditorium on company premises with comfortable seating (on the third floor at headquarters so no one needs to travel to get there).

PREPARATION

1. CHOOSE YOUR DESTINATION.

Howard sat down and grabbed a large sheet of paper. He drummed his fingers on the desk, *Where to begin?*

He started to think about his audience. Who were they? Difficult question to answer, given that the majority of the company would be there. They were made up of a cross-section of managers dying to know the secrets of getting a project done to new recruits with little idea of why they were attending.

When thinking about what they want to know, Howard kept coming back to the managers. They wanted to know how to get a project implemented without the usual stalling and focus on the status quo they were normally confronted with. Whenever they wanted to rollout a new project or make some change to improve the business, they were faced with the same old problem, an established group of mid-level employees who poo-pooed anything likely to "change the way things are always done." Given that this was the only prevailing "want" from his audience, Howard noted this on his sheet of paper.

Howard considered what the audience would need to know. For the managers, they needed to know how to push through a change diplomatically. This meant they needed to expect, and be prepared for, common stalling tactics. For the others in the audience who were just interested to hear about the project, or weren't sure why they were there, Howard figured they needed to know these tactics too. It would help them with their future projects and careers, after all.

The more he thought about it, the more Howard realized that he wanted to make a radical change at his company. No one should have to go through the pain he experienced just to get a project done. He wanted to blow-up this entrenched status-quo system and help everyone to push forward with positive change. To this end, he needed his audience to be ready to do some evaluation following his presentation. Audience members with failed projects under their belts should evaluate what went wrong. What derailed the project? Could they have used Howard's experience to push their project through? What is the likelihood that they could resurrect it? Audience members who haven't experienced the excitement of a new project, only to have it end up on the not-going-anywhere bonfire should think about change they want to take.

CHECKLIST:

- Destination: Evaluate a failed project or potential project from Howard's perspective.

"I was sitting in my office thinking about my stalled project. Thinking about what I was going to report to the executives who thought their project was progressing and expecting to see a surge in sales as a result. What could I say to them? I had failed miserably. Years of service to Intatech, and I couldn't push a project through. Maybe it was time to look for another job. Should I quit?

"And then I had an idea. At that moment, when I was thinking about quitting, considering throwing away years of service, I remembered something. Every time I've had a project meeting, to try and get the buy-in from others, there had been discussions about people quitting.

"Most of my meetings turned ugly pretty quickly. Staff and managers alike complained openly, and often threatened to quit. The prospect of change really shook people up. As I sat there and thought back to all those ugly meetings, something became clear... The longer someone had worked for the organization, the more upset they were.

"And then it hit me!... What if the longer someone had worked for the company, the more jaded they became? What if the longer they worked for the company, the more they felt they weren't being listened to? And that's when everything changed.

"From that point on, I focused my project meetings on asking questions. Instead of being the know-it-all anointed by the executives to implement the special project, I chose to be the listener, the person seeking everyone's help, wisdom, and advice to make my project work. Previously, I'd been pushing people to buy in on my project, basically telling them to agree with me. Now, I was the guy saying, '*I need help, and I want to listen to your experience to work out the best way of doing the project.*'

"Something amazing happened... Instantly...

"Everyone wanted to support me! No more fighting. No more beating my head against the wall. I'd gone to them, cap in hand, and they were falling over themselves to help me and my team. All of a sudden, my project went from making no progress to being on schedule and eventually ahead of schedule.

"So, here's what I found out. Despite the active inertia our organization has lolled around in for the last 10 or 20 years, we can make positive change. You can add value to the company with your change initiatives. You can get support for your ideas. You can feel good about yourself and the contribution you're making every day.

"You can add value if you value others. Show others that you value their opinions and ideas, and don't act like a know-it-all.

"Together, we can make Intatech number one in the market again. Every one of you can add value by showing how much you value others. I urge you to initiate your change ideas and resurrect those long-forgotten projects. We can do it together. Thank you."

CHECKLIST:

- Destination: Evaluate a failed project or potential project from Howard's perspective.

- Knowledge: Review not only the core materials, but also extraneous items that may be interest to your audience.

- Map: Projects; 1. Business Problem; 2. My Project; 3. Overcome Challenges; 4. Value.

- Frame: How to have an impact on your organization.

- First rehearsal: Practice delivering your speech without notes or cues (leveraging your Presentation Path as a recall device).

6. SLIDES

Having practiced his talk, Howard was feeling much better about the presentation. He was comfortable talking about his topic, the Presentation Path was easy to remember, and he was pretty sure the audience would be engaged with what he had to say. He actually felt that he could get away without using slides, but by adding some, he could give his presentation a little more punch, simply by emphasizing key points.

Below is Howard's practiced speech along with slides as they would appear during his talk:

"Please raise your hand if you want to feel good about yourself when you start work in the morning and when you go home in the evening.

"Please keep your hand raised if having an impact, making a positive contribution to the organization, would help you feel good about yourself.

"Today, I'm going to show you how you can make a positive contribution, you can feel good about yourself, and you can secure your future. And I'm going to do all of this within the next 30 minutes, so you don't want to miss a second of what I'm about to share.

"I'd like to tell you a story. About a disease our organization suffers from and how it almost drove me to quit. I'll show you how I turned things around and avoided having to look for another job. Finally, I'll give you a present. I'm going to show you how you can do good and feel good.

"Let me first put on my doctor's cap and tell you about a terrible disease. It's a disease which is difficult to cure. A disease that, left untreated, will spiral out of control. Our company suffers from this disease and has done for many years. It prevents our growth. It hobbles our competitiveness. It's called active inertia.

"Active inertia causes us to look backwards. Instead of trying to change and adapt, we replicate what's happened in the past. That's what we've been doing for years, and it has damaged our position in the market.

"When we're faced with a challenge, like a new competitor, we always choose the wrong path. It's the easy path. It's the path of least resistance. It's the wrong path. Instead of innovating and looking to outsmart the competitor, we go back to what worked 10 years ago and try more of that. We pooh-pooh new ideas, we resist change. Our competitors gallop ahead...

"We fall behind.

"And even though we're working hard internally, we continue to slide.

"While we ramp up 20-year-old sales campaigns, our profits dive.

"For anyone trying to implement innovative change, it is always a frustrating experience. At every turn, we're met with roadblocks. Naysayers claim that the different strategy doesn't work. Stay with the old, the tried and tested, they say...

"Meanwhile, a larger and larger pile of unfinished projects gathers in the trash can of dead aspirations.

"I was a victim too.

"I was asked by the executives to implement a new sales campaign. A tiered sales system that would be a challenging project even if there was no resistance to change. A project that, if it worked as expected, would see a massive boost in sales and a turnaround in customer attrition.

"Well, it was a nightmare from the get-go.

"From the start of the project, there was passive and active resistance. No one wanted to make the change. Accounting didn't want to change. Sales didn't want to change. Operations did everything in their power to get the project stopped. And keep in mind, this was a project sponsored by the executives. And still, no one would even give it a chance.

"Long nights without any sleep and long days that felt like I was beating my head against a wall and getting nowhere. No one would touch anything to do with my project, and time was fast running out.

"I was sitting in my office thinking about my stalled project. Thinking about what I was going to report to the executives who thought their project was progressing and expecting to see a surge in sales as a result. What could I say to them? I had failed miserably. Years of service to Intatech, and I couldn't push a project through. Maybe it was time to look for another job. Should I quit?

"And then, I had an idea.

"At that moment, when I was thinking about quitting, considering throwing away years of service, I remembered something. Every time I've had a project meeting, to try and get buy-in from others, there had been discussions about people quitting.

"Most of my meetings turned ugly pretty quickly. Staff and managers alike complained openly and often threatened to quit. The prospect of change really shook people up. As I sat there and thought back to all those ugly meetings, something became clear... The longer someone had worked for the organization, the more upset they were.

"And then it hit me!... What if the longer someone had worked for the company, the more jaded they became? What if the longer they worked for the company, the more they felt they weren't being listened to? And that's when everything changed.

"From that point on, I focused my project meetings on asking questions. Instead of being the know-it-all anointed by the executives to implement the special project, I chose to be the listener, the person seeking everyone's help, wisdom, and advice to make my project work. Previously, I'd been pushing people to buy in on my project, basically telling them to agree with me. Now, I was the guy saying, '*I need help, and I want to listen to your experience to work out the best way of doing the project.*'

"Something amazing happened... Instantly...

"Everyone wanted to support me! No more fighting. No more beating my head against the wall. I'd gone to them, cap in hand, and they were falling over themselves to help me and my team. All of a sudden, my project went from making no progress to being on schedule and eventually ahead of schedule.

"So, here's what I found out. Despite the active inertia our organization has lolled around in for the last 10 or 20 years, we can make positive change. You can add value to the company with your change initiatives. You can get  support for your ideas. You can feel good about yourself and the contribution you're making every day.

"You can add value if you value others. Show others that you value their opinions and ideas, and don't act like a know-it-all.

"Together, we can make Intatech number one in the market again. Every one of you can add value by showing how much you value others. I urge you to initiate your change ideas and resurrect those long-forgotten projects. We can do it together. Thank you."

David McGimpsey

CHECKLIST:

- Destination: Evaluate a failed project or potential project from Howard's perspective.

- Knowledge: Review not only the core materials, but also extraneous items that may be of interest to your audience.

- Map: Projects; 1. Business Problem; 2. My Project; 3. Overcome Challenges; 4. Value.

- Frame: How to have an impact on your organization

- First rehearsal: Practice delivering your speech without notes or cues (leveraging your Presentation Path as a recall device).

- Slides: Design slides that complement and add impact to your speech.

7. DRESS REHEARSAL

Howard's dress rehearsal was simple. A matter of practicing again with the addition of his slides. His first practice didn't go so smoothly simply due to timing, but on his second and third attempts, his timing was better, and he was able to deliver without looking back at the projected slides.

Howard was ready to deliver live!

12

WHERE TO NOW?

Whether you're about to do your first presentation or your 500th, you can improve. You can improve your confidence, your credibility, your story-telling, your power to engage an audience, your question handling, and your slide design. But, you have to be willing to try something different. You have to be willing to try an approach that seems foreign. An approach that, while possibly feels clunky at first, will become second-nature and will save you time in the long-run.

I wish you all the best on your journey to deliver outstanding presentations. As part of this journey, I invite you to join me and thousands of others in the fight against bad presentations at www.presentationblogger.com

I look forward to hearing about your success!

Your friend,

David McGimpsey (Dave Mac)

Osaka, Japan

www.presentationblogger.com

Made in the USA
Columbia, SC
03 December 2017